W9-BKE-915

# Invertebrates

# Snails, Clams, and Their Relatives

Mollusks

Beth Blaxland
for the Australian Museum

CHELSEA HOUSE
PUBLISHERS
A Haights Cross Communications Company
Philadelphia

Chelsea House Publishers
1974 Sproul Road, Suite 400
Broomall, PA 19008-0914

The Chelsea House world wide web address is www.chelseahouse.com

Library of Congress Cataloging-in-Publication Data Applied for.
ISBN 0-7910-6997-4

First published in 2002 by
MACMILLAN EDUCATION AUSTRALIA PTY LTD
627 Chapel St, South Yarra, Australia, 3141

Edited by Anna Fern
Text design by Polar Design Pty Ltd
Cover design by Polar Design Pty Ltd
Illustrations by Peter Mather, Watershed Art and Design
Australian Museum Publishing Unit: Jenny Saunders and Kate Lowe
Australian Museum Series Editor: Deborah White
Australian Museum Scientific Adviser: Ian Loch

Printed in China

**Acknowledgements**
Cover photograph: Sea snail, courtesy of Steven David Miller/Nature Focus.

C. Andrew Henley/Nature Focus, p. 13; Carl Bento/Nature Focus, p. 14; Clay Bryce/Lochman Transparencies, pp. 5 (top), 6, 8 (all), 17 (top), 21 (top), 22 (bottom), 23, 26 (bottom, left), 30; Dennis Sarson/Lochman Transparencies, p. 12; Jay Sarson/Lochman Transparencies, p. 28; Jiri Lochman/Transparencies, pp. 15, 24 (top), 26 (top), (bottom, left); Karen Gowlett-Holmes/Nature Focus, pp. 4, 7 (top & bottom), 11 (all), 17 (top), 18 (bottom), 19, 20, 21 (bottom), 22 (top), 29; Michael Aw/Nature Focus, pp. 5 (bottom) 7, 18 (top); Steven David Miller/Nature Focus, pp. 3, 9, 16; Steve Wilson/Lochman Transparencies, pp. 24 (bottom), 25.

While every care has been taken to trace and acknowledge copyright, the publisher tenders their apologies for any accidental infringement where copyright has proved untraceable.

# Contents

**Glossary words**

When a word is printed in **bold**, you can look up its meaning in the Glossary on page 31.

# What are mollusks?

Mollusks are a group of invertebrate animals. An invertebrate is an animal that does not have a backbone. There are many different kinds of invertebrates. Some other examples of invertebrates are spiders, sea stars and worms. Can you think of any other invertebrates?

There are many different kinds of mollusks. Most mollusks live in the sea, but some live on land and some live in **freshwater** ponds, lakes and streams. The main kinds of mollusks are:

◎ snails and slugs

◎ chitons

◎ bivalves (which include clams and cockle shells)

◎ cephalopods (which include octopuses and squids).

### Did you know

Sometimes empty seashells are washed up onto beaches. These shells were made by sea snails and other mollusks that live in the sea. Mollusks grow these shells around their bodies and leave them behind when they die.

### Fascinating fact

Mollusks are one of the biggest groups of invertebrates. There are about 100,000 different types of mollusks.

▼ **A sea slug is a mollusk.**

# General features of mollusks

Some kinds of mollusks look very different from other kinds of mollusks. For example, a snail looks very different from an octopus. Scientists put these different-looking animals into the same group because they are all closely related. Scientists know these animals are closely related because their bodies all have the same general features.

> **A snail is a mollusk. Most mollusks crawl on a muscle called a foot.**

Snails, slugs, chitons, clams, cockles, octopuses and squids are all mollusks because they are all invertebrates that have:

◎ a soft body

◎ a **mantle** which is a section of skin that often grows a shell

◎ a strong muscle under their body that they use for moving about. Most mollusks crawl on a long, flat muscle called a **foot**. Some mollusks, such as octopuses and squids, swim using a tube-shaped muscle called a **funnel**.

> **An octopus is a mollusk. Some mollusks have a tube-shaped muscle called a funnel.**

funnel

## How do you say it?

| | |
|---|---|
| bivalves: | *by*-valvs |
| cephalopods: | *sef*-al-o-pods |
| chitons: | *kite*-ons |
| invertebrate: | in-*vert*-a-bret |
| mantle: | *man*-tl |
| mollusks: | *mol*-usks |

# Mollusk bodies

Mollusks have a soft body. The bodies of most mollusks have three parts: a head, a foot and a visceral mass. The visceral mass is the part of the body that contains the stomach and other body organs.

Many mollusks have a shell to protect their soft body. The shell grows from a special part of the mollusk's skin called the mantle. Different kinds of mollusks grow shells that are different sizes, shapes and colors.

The bodies of snails and slugs, chitons, bivalves and cephalopods each look a little different.

**How do you say it?**

visceral:  *viss*-er-al

## Snails and slugs

A snail or slug has a head with eyes, **tentacles** and a mouth. A long, flat foot joins onto the back of the head and is used for creeping about. The visceral mass lies on top of the foot. Many snails and slugs have a single shell that covers all or part of their visceral mass.

Ⓥ **This is a snail.**

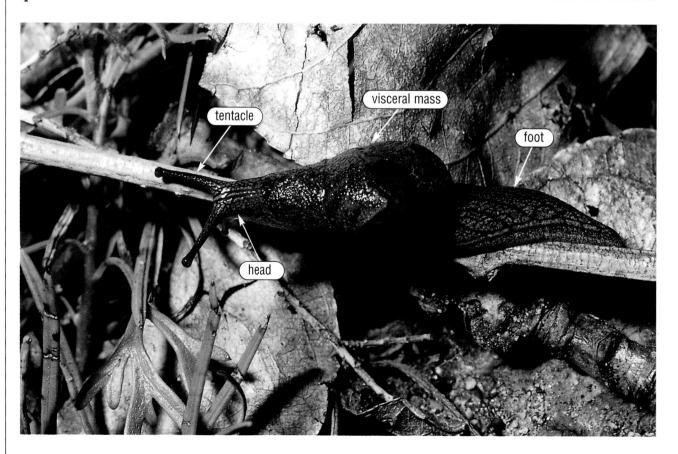

tentacle

visceral mass

foot

head

## Chitons

A chiton has a flat body with an oval shape. It has a tiny head with a mouth, but it does not have eyes or tentacles. The head joins onto a wide, flat foot. The visceral mass lies above the foot. All chitons have a small, flat shell with eight parts.

## Bivalves

A bivalve has a narrow body that lies inside a shell with two parts. The two parts join together on one side and the bivalve can open and close its shell like a book. The visceral mass and foot lie inside the shell, but there is no head.

**Did you know** ❓

A bivalve is the only kind of mollusk that does not have a head.

⋀ **A chiton has a flat body under a small shell with eight parts. It clings tightly onto rocks with its wide, flat foot.**

## Fascinating fact

A cephalopod swims by squirting water through its funnel. It can swim forwards or backwards. If it squirts a jet of water behind its body, its body is pushed forwards. If it squirts a jet of water forwards, its body is pushed backwards.

⋀ **These are bivalves.**

## Cephalopods

Most cephalopods have eight strong arms. Many also have two long tentacles. The arms and tentacles join onto one side of the head. Their visceral mass joins onto the other side of the head. Cephalopods also have a large tube called a funnel that helps them swim.

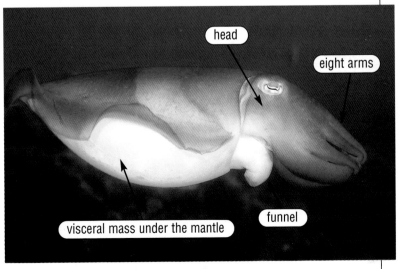

head

eight arms

visceral mass under the mantle

funnel

⋀ **This is a cephalopod.**

# Special features of mollusk bodies

## Shells

Many mollusks have a shell, but some do not. Mollusks without a shell include octopuses and some slugs. Some mollusks, such as bivalves, and many snails have a shell that is large enough to fit their whole body inside. Other mollusks, such as chitons and some snails, slugs and cephalopods, have a small shell. These shells are often flat and sit on top of the mollusks' bodies. Sometimes the shell is hard to see because it is partly or fully covered by the mantle.

◀ **This cowry is a kind of snail. Cowries often stretch their mantle out to cover part of their shell.**

shell

mantle

▽ **A chiton's small shell is made of eight plates that line up in a row along its back. The plates are held together by skin.**

A snail's shell is always made in one piece, but some mollusks have shells with two or more parts. A bivalve's shell is always made up of two curved parts called valves. The two valves have a hinge on one side that lets it open and close. A chiton's shell is always made up of eight flat parts called plates. The eight plates line up in a row along the chiton's back. The shell is too small to cover all of the chiton, and so its body bulges out below the shell.

A young mollusk has a tiny body and a tiny shell. As the mollusk's body grows bigger, the shell grows too. New shell grows around the edges of the shell's opening to make the shell bigger. The oldest parts of the shell are tiny. The oldest part of a bivalve's shell is closest to where the two valves join together. The oldest part of a snail's shell is the part where the spiral is smallest. Bigger spirals grow as the snail's body grows.

This is the oldest part of the snail's shell.

Ⓥ If a snail has a shell with a spiral shape, you can find out if it is right-handed or left-handed by looking at its shell. Hold the shell so that the opening faces towards you and the end with the smallest spirals points upwards. A right-handed snail grows a shell that opens on the right side. A left-handed snail grows a shell that opens on the left side. Most kinds of snails are right-handed, but some kinds are left-handed.

Ⓐ The oldest part of a snail's shell is the part where the spiral is smallest. Bigger spirals are needed as the body grows bigger.

Did you know ?

Some snails are right-handed and some are left-handed, even though they do not have any hands!

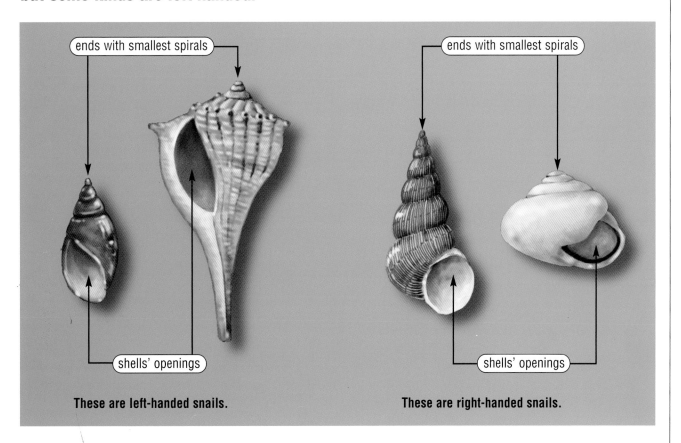

ends with smallest spirals

ends with smallest spirals

shells' openings

shells' openings

**These are left-handed snails.**

**These are right-handed snails.**

# The life cycles of mollusks

**M**ollusks make new mollusks through sexual reproduction. The adult female provides eggs and the adult male provides **sperm**. When an egg and a sperm join, a new mollusk begins to grow. Snails, slugs, chitons, bivalves and cephalopods all **reproduce** in this way.

Mollusks have two main kinds of life cycle. In one kind of life cycle, the young mollusks first grow into **larvae** that swim about in the water. The larvae look very different from their parents. Later, the larvae change to look like tiny adults. The other kind of life cycle does not produce swimming larvae. When these young mollusks hatch, they already look like their parents.

## A life cycle with swimming larvae

Most mollusks that live in the sea and many that live in fresh water have a life cycle that includes swimming larvae.

To reproduce, an adult female provides eggs and an adult male provides sperm. Most bivalves, most chitons and some snails release their eggs and sperm into the water at about the same time and place. Some male snails and slugs place their sperm inside the female's body, near her eggs.

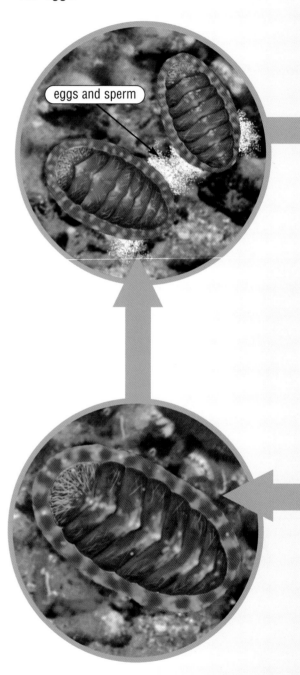

eggs and sperm

Many of these young mollusks become adults when they are between six months and five years old. The adult mollusks are then ready to reproduce.

When the egg and sperm join, a larva begins to grow. The larva is so tiny that a **microscope** is needed to see it. The larva swims about in the water and looks very different from adult mollusks. As a larva gets bigger, it starts to grow a tiny foot and shell.

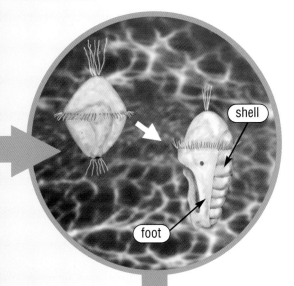

shell

foot

 Some sea snails lay their eggs in special egg cases which help protect the growing larvae. This picture shows a group of clear egg cases filled with many hundreds of tiny purple eggs.

## Did you know ❓

Slug larvae grow tiny shells but, when they change into adults, some kinds of slugs lose their shells and never grow them back.

After a few weeks or months, the larva's body changes to look like a tiny adult. This young mollusk is very tiny.

## How do you say it?

larva:        *lar-va*
larvae:       *lar-vee*

 There are two adult chitons and many young chitons on this rock.

# A life cycle without swimming larvae

Some mollusks have a different kind of life cycle. These mollusks do not produce larvae that swim about in water. Instead, their eggs hatch into young mollusks that already look like the adults. Mollusks that have this kind of life cycle include the snails and slugs that live on land, some kinds of sea snails and sea slugs, and most cephalopods.

To reproduce, an adult female provides eggs and an adult male provides sperm. The males place their sperm inside the female, near her eggs. Male cephalopods use one of their arms to place their sperm inside the female's body. Male snails use their penis to place sperm inside the female's body. A snail's penis is found at the back of its head, just behind its right tentacle. When it needs to, the snail can stretch its penis into a long tube. Then it puts its penis into a special hole at the back of the female's head.

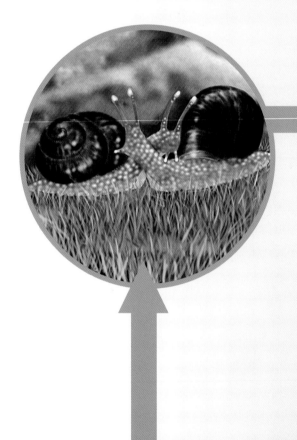

 **Many snails that live on land lay eggs that are big enough to be easily seen.**

## Did you know ❓

Some kinds of sea slugs live for only a few weeks, but some bivalves live for more than 30 years.

The egg and sperm join inside the mother's body and a new mollusk begins to grow. Some kinds of mollusks grow the young mollusks inside their bodies. Other mollusks lay eggs that hatch later. These eggs are often big enough to be easily seen. Some large land snails from South America and Africa even lay eggs that are more than 1 inch (2.5 centimeters) wide! When the mother gives birth or the eggs hatch, the new mollusks look like tiny adults. These young mollusks are very small, but they can be seen without using a microscope.

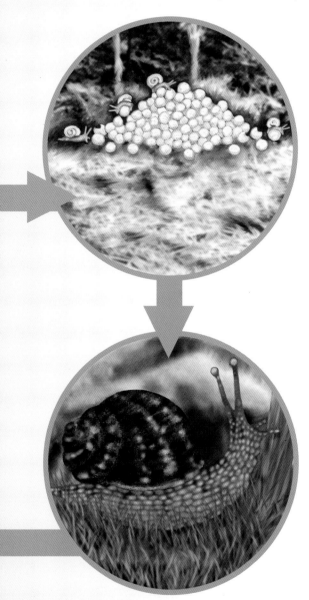

▼ **When a land snail's eggs hatch, the young snails come out looking like tiny adults.**

Many of these young mollusks become adults when they are between six months and two years old, but some cephalopods can take four years to mature. The adult mollusks are then ready to reproduce.

# Where mollusks live

Mollusks live in many places all around the world. Most mollusks live in the sea, but some mollusks live in freshwater ponds, lakes or streams. Some mollusks live on land.

▽ **These are freshwater mussels.**

## Fresh water

Some mollusks live in the fresh water found in many ponds, lakes, dams, streams and rivers. The only mollusks that live in fresh water are some kinds of snails and some bivalves such as freshwater mussels and clams. Snails crawl about on the bottom or on plants growing in the water. Most of the bivalves live where they can burrow into soft sand or mud on the bottom.

## Land

The only mollusks that live on land are some kinds of snails and slugs. Different kinds of snails and slugs live in different land **habitats**. These habitats include rainforests, woodlands, grasslands and gardens. Most land snails and slugs prefer places that are cool and moist. They often burrow in moist soil or seek shelter under fallen logs, bark or leaves on the ground. Some snails even live in dry deserts, but they only move about after rain or at night when it is cool.

 **There are many different kinds of land snails.**

## The sea

Mollusks live in seas all around the world. They can be found everywhere, from the deepest parts of the sea to the seashore. All chitons and cephalopods and most bivalves, snails and slugs live in the sea. Different kinds of mollusks live in different sea habitats. Many mollusks live on or in the sea floor. Some mollusks prefer to live in places where the sea floor is hard. Others prefer to live in places where the sea floor is soft. There are also some mollusks that live in the open sea.

## Hard sea floors

Hard sea floors are made of rock or **coral**. Mollusks that live on hard sea floors include many kinds of snails, slugs and chitons, and some bivalves and cephalopods. Many of these mollusks move about over the sea floor. For example, octopuses crawl over the sea floor. They have suckers on their arms to help them crawl up and over rocks and corals. Other mollusks, such as adult rock oysters, always stay in the one place. A rock oyster is a bivalve that attaches its shell onto a rock and cannot move about.

⚠ **This triton is a large sea snail that can be found crawling on rocks and coral reefs.**

Many mollusks live on rocky seashores at the edge of the sea. This habitat is covered by sea water at **high tide** but is dry at **low tide**. At high tide, the rocks are covered by sea water and sea snails, and chitons crawl about under the water. At low tide, the snails and chitons sit still and rest.

### Fascinating fact

Some sea snails called limpets always go back to exactly the same place to rest at low tide. This is called their home. A limpet's home is a very shallow hole in the rock that is just the right size and shape for its body to sit in and its shell to cover.

## Soft sea floors

Soft sea floors are made of sand or mud. Mollusks that live on soft sea floors include some snails, slugs and bivalves. Some of these mollusks live on the surface of the sand or mud, and some live on seagrasses that grow there. Others burrow into the soft ground. Most of the mollusks that burrow live just below the surface, but some dig deep burrows.

▶ **This bivalve is called a scallop. When it is not swimming about, it sits on the sea floor where it often covers itself with sand.**

**Did you know** ❓

Some large bivalves dig burrows that are more than 3 feet (1 meter) deep.

tentacles on the mantle

edge of the shell

mantle

## The open sea

Some kinds of mollusks prefer to live in the open sea, where they swim and float in the water. Mollusks that live in the open sea include some snails and slugs, and many cephalopods. Some of these mollusks swim through the water and others float on top of the water. Mollusks that swim include cephalopods such as squids and cuttlefishes. Most cephalopods swim by squirting water through their funnels. Mollusks that float include some sea slugs and sea snails. These mollusks use bubbles of air to help them float.

**Fascinating fact**

Many adult mollusks live on the sea floor, but the larvae of these mollusks float and swim near the surface of the sea.

⬆ **This violet snail can float using air bubbles it makes with its foot.**

# How mollusks sense the world

△ **Most sea snails have two tentacles on their heads. They use their tentacles to feel and smell. Their eyes are found at the bottom of these tentacles.**

**M**ollusks use their senses to find out about the world around them. They use their senses to find food, the right habitat and shelter. Their senses also help them escape from danger. Most mollusks have simple eyes and tentacles that help them sense their surroundings. They also sense things with other parts of their bodies.

## Touch

All mollusks have the sense of touch. Mollusks feel things with their skin, and many have special tentacles that they use to explore their surroundings.

## Smell

Most mollusks can smell or sense chemicals in their surroundings. Being able to smell helps mollusks find their food. Mollusks smell things through their tentacles or through their skin. Snails, slugs and bivalves smell with their tentacles. Cephalopods smell through the skin on their arms and tentacles. Chitons smell things through their mantle.

### Did you know ❓

Tiny tentacles are found on the foot and mantle of some snails, slugs and bivalves. Most snails and slugs also have long tentacles on their heads. Some snails and slugs have two long tentacles on their heads, but others have four.

◁ **Some of a bivalve's sense organs are on its mantle, near the edge of its shell. Bivalves have many tentacles that can smell and feel. Some bivalves, such as this scallop, also have many small blue eyes.**

# Light

Most snails and slugs, and some bivalves and chitons, have simple eyes. These eyes can only sense light or dark. They cannot see shapes or colors.

Cephalopods have eyes that can see quite well. They can see the shapes of things around them. Cephalopods' eyes help them find and hunt animals to eat.

Some mollusks, such as chitons, sense light with their skin. They use this sense to help them find places in the shade where they can hide.

Ⓥ **Land snails, and some sea snails like this one, have four tentacles on their heads. Their eyes are found on the ends of two of these tentacles. This sea snail is curled up in its shell and watching for danger.**

# Gravity

Many mollusks can sense **gravity**. This sense lets them know which way is up and which way is down. Most mollusks cannot see very well, so this sense helps them know if their body is facing upwards, downwards or sideways. Mollusks that do not move about, such as oysters, do not have this sense.

# What mollusks eat

Different mollusks eat different kinds of foods. Some mollusks are filter feeders. These mollusks live in water and eat tiny plants, animals and pieces of food floating in the water. Other mollusks eat larger animals or plants.

## Filter feeders

Most bivalves are filter feeders. They eat tiny plants and animals, called **plankton**, that they filter out of the water. Bivalves that live on hard sea floors filter food out of the water around them. Many bivalves that burrow in sand or mud have special tubes that help them get their food. The bivalve stays under the sand or mud and stretches its tubes up into the water. One tube sucks water into the shell where the food is gathered. The other tube takes the water back out of the shell.

### Did you know

Filter feeders can eat only when they are under water. Some filter feeders, such as rock oysters, live on the seashore and are left out of the water at low tide. When they are out of the water, they cannot eat, so they close their shells. When the tide comes in and they are covered by water again, they open their shells and start feeding.

The frilly opening of this tube helps to keep sand out when it sucks in water and food.

▶ **Some bivalves burrow under the sand and stretch little tubes up into the water to filter feed.**

# Plant and animal eaters

Mollusks that eat plants or animals have a special kind of tongue called a radula. The radula is covered with many rows of sharp teeth. It helps mollusks to gather and eat their food.

## Plant eaters

Chitons and some snails and slugs eat seaweeds, freshwater plants or garden plants. Some use their radula to scrape small plants into their mouths. Others use their radula to cut bigger plants into small pieces they can swallow.

**▶ This sea hare is a kind of sea slug that eats the tiny seaweeds that grow on rocks on the sea floor.**

**⬆ These whelks have found the head of a dead fish to eat. These sea snails use their senses of smell and taste to find the dead and rotting animals they like to eat.**

## Animal eaters

Many snails eat other animals. Some snails graze on corals and other invertebrate animals that cannot move about. Some snails are predators that hunt and kill animals to eat, and some snails are scavengers that find and eat dead animals. They eat animals such as worms, slugs, bivalves and other snails. Some of these snails cut their food into small pieces with their radula. Other snails use their radula like a spear to stab and catch their food. Most cephalopods are predators. Their eyes are very good at finding fish and invertebrates such as crabs. They catch their **prey** with their tentacles or arms, and then bite off pieces to swallow.

## Fascinating fact

Some mollusks have a radula with only 16 teeth, but most have hundreds or thousands of teeth. The tooth-covered radula is always growing forwards. This brings new, sharp teeth towards the front of the mouth, where they replace the old, blunt ones that fall out.

## How do you say it?

radula: *rad-yoo-la*

# How mollusks defend themselves

Many mollusks protect their soft bodies by curling up inside a large shell. Some mollusks do not have a large shell for protection. These mollusks have other ways to defend themselves.

## Shells

Shells help protect mollusks from predators and harsh surroundings. For example, many sea snails and chitons live in places where strong waves crash onto the seashore. These mollusks have strong shells to protect their soft bodies from being crushed.

Mollusks also need to protect their bodies from drying out. Some mollusks live in places that can become very dry. These mollusks curl up inside their shells and plug the openings. They wait until the high tide covers them or until it rains, then they open their shells up again.

⋀ A big shell can protect a mollusk's soft body. This cone shell also uses a dart in its mouth to inject a poison. Some cone shells are so poisonous they can kill a person.

## Scaring predators

Some mollusks can scare away predators. Most cephalopods and some sea snails and sea slugs scare predators by quickly changing their body color. They flash bright colored patterns to frighten their predators away.

Some sea slugs have skin that is poisonous, tastes horrible or stings. These mollusks scare away experienced predators that have encountered the sea slugs before.

◁ Many sea slugs have poisonous skin.

# Hiding

Mollusks that do not have a large shell are often very hard to find. Many of these mollusks hide from their predators. They hide under plants and rocks or in soil, mud or sand. Most mollusks hide during the day and come out to feed only at night. Many mollusks also use camouflage to hide from predators. This means their bodies have colors and patterns that look like their surroundings and make them hard to see.

ⓥ **This cowry shell is crawling over a soft coral and is hard to see in these surroundings.**

# Escaping

Cephalopods and some other mollusks can quickly swim away from predators. Many cephalopods also squirt out a brown or black liquid called ink. This turns the water black so the predator cannot see the cephalopod, helping the cephalopod to escape. Some sea slugs are able to escape from predators by breaking off bits of their mantle or other parts of their bodies.

There are thousands of different kinds of land snails around the world. They live in different land habitats, but prefer places that are warm and damp. They can be found in rainforests, woodlands, gardens, farmland and even in some deserts.

The brown garden snail is the land snail that many people know best. It has a gray body and a shell with a light and dark brown pattern and is often seen in gardens. Its shell can grow up to 1.5 inches (4 centimeters) long, but its body can stretch even longer.

Most land snails are much smaller than the brown garden snail. Many have a shell smaller than one-half inch (1 centimeter) high. Some land snails are very large. Some giant land snails from Africa have a shell that is 11 inches (27 centimeters) high.

These small snails are fully grown.

◬ **Two different kinds of land snail are shown in this picture.**

Some land snails eat plants. Brown garden snails and giant land snails from Africa eat some garden flowers, vegetables and fruits. Many people do not like these snails because they can kill young plants and ruin crops. Some land snails eat invertebrate animals such as earthworms and slugs, or even other snails.

◀ **Giant land snails from Africa are a pest in many countries because they eat plants that people grow.**

## Fascinating fact

One kind of giant land snail from Africa lays eggs that are 1 inch (2.5 centimeters) wide. They are so big that people sometimes think they are birds' eggs.

# snails

When a land snail moves around, it leaves a slimy trail. The slime is called mucus. The sticky, wet mucus is made in the snail's skin. The mucus keeps the snail's body wet and helps it crawl on its foot.

Many land snails shelter during the day and come out only at night or after rain. If their surroundings become very dry or very cold, the snails curl up inside their shells and close the openings. Then they stay very still and wait until it rains or warms up. Some snails hide from predators first. They burrow into the ground or climb up a tree or a wall to hide from predators on the ground.

## Fascinating fact

There are two ways that a land snail can close the opening of its shell. Most land snails plug the opening with mucus. At first the mucus is soft, but it becomes hard when it dries. Some land snails have a hard, round disc on top of their foot. When the snail pulls its body inside its shell, it bends its foot so that the disc covers the opening.

## How do you say it?

escargots: *es-kar-**go***
mucus: ***mew**-kus*

 **These snails have climbed up off the ground and curled up inside their shells to wait for better weather.**

## Did you know ?

Some people like to eat land snails. When someone goes to a restaurant and orders *escargots*, they want to eat cooked snails.

Pearls are a gem that people make into expensive necklaces and other jewelry. Pearls can be made by many kinds of mollusks, but the best pearls are made by special kinds of bivalves called pearl oysters.

To make a pearl, something such as a grain of sand has to get caught between the mollusk's mantle and shell. The inside layer of a mollusk's shell is usually very smooth. If sand gets stuck between the mantle and shell, it scratches the mollusk's soft body. The mantle grows shell over the grain of sand to keep its body from being scratched. When the shell grows over and around the sand, it makes a pearl.

Some people dive down to the sea floor to collect wild pearl oysters. Then they help the oysters grow large, round pearls by placing a small, round object between the pearl oyster's mantle and shell for it to grow shell around. The pearl oysters are kept in pearl farms in the sea. After about two years, the oyster is opened and the pearl is taken out and sold.

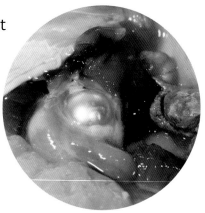

Ⓥ This oyster is growing a shiny white pearl between its shell and soft body.

Ⓥ These pearl oysters are from a pearl farm. They are kept in special cages in the sea where the oyster can keep feeding and growing.

## Did you know ?

Pearls can have many shapes and colors. They can be round like a ball, half-round with a flat base and round top, shaped like a teardrop, or any other shape. Pearls can be white, pale pink or yellow. They can also be dark blue, purple, brown, gray or black.

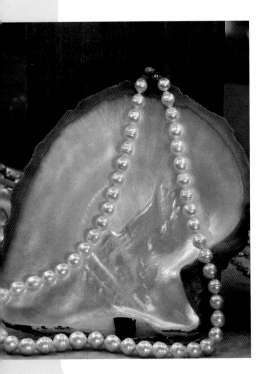

◂ This pearl necklace is lying on half of a pearl oyster's shell. The inside layer of the shell is made of the same material as the pearls.

# oysters

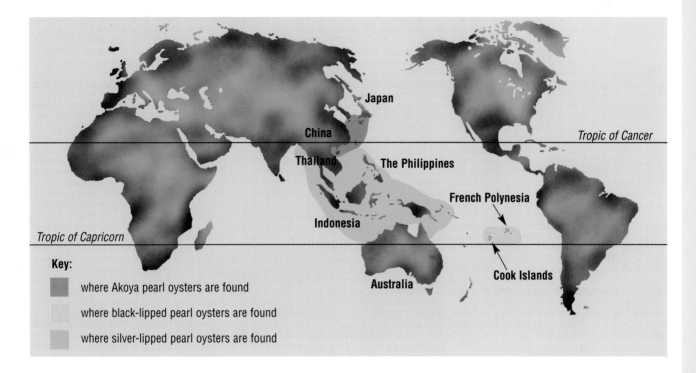

Key:
- where Akoya pearl oysters are found
- where black-lipped pearl oysters are found
- where silver-lipped pearl oysters are found

There are many different kinds of pearl oysters around the world. Some of these are the Akoya pearl oyster, the black-lipped pearl oyster and the silver-lipped pearl oyster. Different kinds of pearl oysters make different kinds of pearls.

The Akoya pearl oyster lives in seas near Japan and China. Its shell grows 5 inches (13 centimeters) long, and it makes small, colored pearls. These are often bleached to make them white.

Most of the pearls from black-lipped pearl oysters come from pearl farms in French Polynesia and the Cook Islands. These are large oysters with shells that are 12 inches (30 centimeters) long. They make big black and dark-colored pearls up to one-half inch (11 millimeters) wide.

Silver-lipped pearl oysters live in the **tropics** in the seas near Australia, Indonesia, Thailand and the Philippines. These oysters grow shells up to 12 inches (30 centimeters) long. They make white and light-colored pearls. The pearl oysters from Australia grow the largest pearls. These pearls can be as big as 1 inch (21 millimeters) wide.

⋀ **Different kinds of pearl oysters are found in different places around the world.**

## Fascinating fact

Some pearl oysters can live for as long as 30 years, but most pearls are produced when the pearl oysters are between 3 and 7 years old.

# Where can you see mollusks?

**M**ollusks can be seen in many gardens and on the seashore. You can also see mollusks or their shells in some museums and in fish shops that sell mussels, cockles, squids and octopuses for people to eat.

## Gardens

Land snails and slugs live in many gardens. They prefer to come out when it is not too hot and dry, and not too cold. The best time to see them is at night or after rain during the warmer parts of the year. If you explore a garden at night, a torch will help you spot these mollusks. Brown garden snails like to eat soft plants, especially seedlings and leafy vegetables such as lettuces. Look on the ground and on plants that have soft leaves and stems.

Some slugs eat leftover dog and cat food. If you have a dog or cat, you could also check in and around their bowls. The best time to see these mollusks is at night.

▶ **These slugs are eating lettuce.**

# The seashore

The seashore is a good place to find chitons, sea snails and bivalves. You might also see a sea slug or an octopus. The best time to explore the seashore is at low tide. Sandy beaches and mud flats are good places to find bivalves and sea snails. On rocky shores, it is easy to see chitons and sea snails. Most chitons hide from the light. To find them, you will need to look in the shade under rock ledges and on rocks close to the water. Many different kinds of sea snails live on the rocks and in rock pools. See how many different ones you can find.

## Did you know

On rocky shores, most mollusks do not move about at low tide. They sit still and wait until the high tide covers them with water before moving about to look for food. In deep rock pools, mollusks are always covered by water. If you look closely, you might see the sea snails slowly moving around. Many are feeding on tiny seaweeds growing on the rock.

**△ Many different kinds of mollusks live on rocky shores and in rock pools.**

## Safety tips

- Make sure that an adult is nearby when you explore rock pools, rocky shores and other seashores. Rocky shores can be dangerous places to explore because the rocks can be slippery and big waves sometimes crash over the rocks. An adult can watch out for these big waves and help you explore safely.

- Some mollusks should not be touched because they can sting or inject poison. Some kinds of cone shells are very dangerous because their poison is strong enough to kill a person.

# Quiz

**1** Is a mollusk an invertebrate? Why?

**2** Which one of the following is not a mollusk?

| | | |
|---|---|---|
| sea snail | cephalopod | chiton |
| sea urchin | bivalve | sea slug |
| land snail | octopus | clam shell |

**3** Which kind of mollusk does not have a head?

**4** Do all mollusks have a shell?

**5** Does a mollusk larva look like its parents?

**6** Where do mollusks live?

**7** How do tentacles help mollusks to sense things around them?

**8** What is a radula?

**9** What does a land snail do if its surroundings become very dry or cold?

**10** When is the best time to look for garden snails?

# Challenge
## QUESTIONS

**1** What is the mantle?

**2** How does a cephalopod swim?

**3** How can you tell if a snail is right-handed or left-handed?

**4** Are a mollusk's eyes always found on the surface of its head?

**5** When a predator comes near, some mollusks defend themselves by quickly changing their body color and flashing bright color patterns. How can this stop the predator from eating it?

Turn to page 32 to check your answers.

**This bivalve is called a spiny oyster. It has a colorful mantle.**

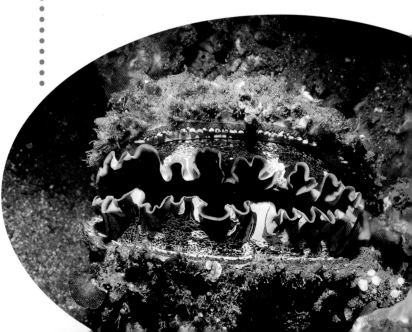

# Glossary

| | |
|---|---|
| corals | Tiny invertebrate animals that live in large groups and make coral reefs. |
| foot | The strong, flat muscle that mollusks such as snails use for crawling about. |
| fresh water | Water that is not salty. |
| funnel | A strong, tube-shaped muscle found under a cephalopod's body. A cephalopod swims by squirting a jet of water through its funnel to push its body along. |
| gravity | The power of Earth to pull things downwards. For example, if you jump up off the ground, gravity pulls you back down. |
| habitat | The place where a living thing, such as a plant or an animal, lives. |
| high tide | When the sea comes in and covers more of the seashore than at low tide. |
| larvae | Young mollusks that live in water. The larvae look very different from the adults. |
| low tide | When the sea goes out and leaves more of the seashore uncovered than at high tide. |
| mantle | A special part of the skin on the top of a mollusk's body that grows its shell. |
| microscope | A special magnifying lens used by scientists to see very tiny things. |
| plankton | Tiny plants and animals in the sea or in fresh water. These include many kinds of invertebrate larvae and adults. |
| prey | Animals that are eaten by other animals. |
| reproduce | To make more of the same kind of animal or plant. |
| sperm | Cells from a male animal's body that can fertilize the eggs from a female animal's body to reproduce. |
| tentacles | Parts of an invertebrate's body that stick out like fingers to sense things or gather food. Tentacles can bend and can often be made longer or shorter. |
| tropics | The part of Earth between the Tropic of Cancer and the Tropic of Capricorn, where air and water temperatures are always warm or hot. |

# Index

## Answers to quiz

1 Yes, because a mollusk is an animal that does not have a backbone.
2 Sea urchin.
3 A bivalve.
4 No. (Octopuses and many adult slugs do not have a shell.)
5 No, a mollusk larva looks very different from its parents.
6 Most mollusks live in the sea, but some live on land and some live in fresh water.
7 Mollusks use their tentacles to feel and smell things. Most land snails' eyes are on the tips of their tentacles, so these mollusks' tentacles also help them to see.
8 A special kind of tongue covered in many rows of sharp teeth.
9 It curls up inside its shell, closes the opening and waits until it rains or warms up.
10 At night or after rain during the warmer parts of the year.

## Answers to challenge questions

1 The special part of a mollusk's skin that often grows a shell.
2 It squirts a jet of water out through its funnel to push its body through the water.
3 Hold the snail's shell so you can see the opening and the smallest spirals at the top. A right-handed snail's shell opens to the right. A left-handed snail's shell opens to the left.
4 No, some mollusks have eyes on other parts of their bodies. Most land snails and land slugs have eyes on the ends of tentacles on their heads. Some bivalves have eyes on their mantle and some chitons have eyes in their shell.
5 The sudden color change scares it away.